Hi
PATTY!.

Peter

CATS of the MASTERS

By Michael Patrick

MJF BOOKS
NEW YORK

Published by MJF Books
Fine Communications
Two Lincoln Square
60 West 66th Street
New York, NY 10023

Cats of the Masters
ISBN 1-56731-335-3

Printed in Singapore
MJF Books and the MJF colophon are trademarks of Fine Creative Media, Inc.

10   9   8   7   6   5   4   3   2   1

INTRODUCTION

CATS OF THE MASTERS

S carce when they are wanted, underfoot when they are not, quick to criticize but soon forgiving, touchy as a diva and serene as a buddha, cats have a way of insinuating their many personalities into every aspect of our lives. From the simple act of reading a newspaper to the more complex undertaking of painting a kitchen chair – or a masterpiece – if there is a cat in the vicinity, you can be sure it will be more a participant than an observer. It should be no surprise, then, that they have found their way into so many of the world's great paintings, seemingly before the artist realized what was going on and painted them out again. When you think of it, who among us *hasn't* had to repaint something – at least once – because of a cat?

The rivalry between Raphael and Michelangelo often degenerated into rampant pranksterism. When Raphael got the mistaken impression that Pope Julius wanted dogs included in the Sistine Chapel frescoes (*see Mutts of the Masters*), Michelangelo happened to overhear the Pope upbraiding him. "Whether you remove them or repaint them I care not. I only know I want to see no dogs in this chapel, and I don't mean maybe." The chastened Raphael reworked the pups into the pensive cherubim with whom we are all familiar. He then went home, sending a message to the Pope. "When next Your Holiness visits the chapel, I guarantee you will see no dogs." By the time the irascible pontiff arrived in the morning, Michelangelo had repainted the panel again, in the version shown here. On his deathbed many years later, Michelangelo said that his only regret, apart from screwing up the *Pietà* so many times, was that he was not present at the next meeting between Raphael and the Pope.

Cats have been favored domestic pets for many centuries – in fact, almost all of recorded history – and the Renaissance was one of their high points. However, even the most ardent keepers of cats know there are certain disadvantages to living in close proximity with *Cattus domesticus*, and this knowledge also apparently has a long history. In illustration, we offer this painting by Botticelli, entitled *Pantheon of the Minor Gods Attempting to Repel or Cover Tuna Breath*.

If the Renaissance was a period of high popularity for the domestic cat, just a few centuries earlier they were widely reviled as harbingers of black magic and demonic possession – and those who disagreed had the Inquisition to think about. It is not surprising, therefore, that the nervous artist (and ipso facto heretic) hid these medieval felines under many layers of gold leaf and paint and, just in case, covered himself further with the Latin inscription *Quid felis?* (What cats?)

In 1962, the most shocking act of vandalism in European history was discovered in the Vatican's Sistine Chapel. Authorities were at a total loss until a statement was released by a splinter religious group who called themselves "The Church of Latterday Freehand Saints," or "Waltists," claiming full credit. The statement explained that they "rejected the traditional Judeo-Christian concept of Jehovah" and, in the interests of religious freedom and equality, had substituted "the true supreme being, Walter." When headlines around the world announced, "Michelangelo Defaced by Cat-Worshiping Cult," the Waltists issued another, much more strongly worded statement: "We resent the implication that we are a bunch of screwballs who deify cats. Our Lord is Walter *Lantz*, Prophet of the Anthropomorphic, Creator of Oswald, and Martyr to the Dark Walt. We demand an apology." Unfortunately, the heat of their indignation made them forget their usual methods of maintaining secrecy. The police traced them through their postmark and the entire Church of LFS was arrested.

For centuries, the *Mona Lisa* has been a symbol of serenity and mysterious beauty. But recently discovered notebooks in da Vinci's handwriting put a different complexion on this most famous of faces. It seems the model, one Myrna Lee Primazetti, was so nervous and fidgety during sittings that Leonardo was obliged to borrow a cat, which he encouraged her to stroke for its calming effect. The cat being a long-haired breed (and snow white), Myrna Lee's black smock was covered with hair by the end of every day's work – and to da Vinci's chagrin, she arrived the next day in the same smock, covered with the same hair, week after week until the portrait was nearly finished. By that time her eyebrows were white with cat hair, leaving the artist no choice but to omit them entirely. "And yet it was for these appendages only," he wrote, "that I wished to paint her from the beginning, so remarkably lush were they as to be not separate entities, but of a piece." The notes include a sketch (far left) of what he had in mind but could never achieve with such a high-strung slob of a model.

One of Rembrandt's most recognizable paintings, *Masters of the Cloth Guild*, is also one of the most controversial. For more than three hundred years, the world has wondered why the guildsmen's attention seems to be focused on empty air. What could they be looking at? Recent expert restorations have finally answered the question – and explained the original title, *Das Geschenk von Hilda zum Burghern* (Hilda's Gift to the Burghers).

Van Gogh painted many views of his modest living quarters in Mme. Escallier's house at Arles. This one he decided to suppress, probably on the grounds that his landlady (known locally as *La Scourge*) would have nailed him for a big deposit, *mais certainement.*

It is not generally known that Matisse's famous representation of goldfish is actually one of a series – and was not produced for purely artistic reasons. Since his goldfish, which he bred carefully and doted on, had disappeared the very morning after his wife's great-aunt Clarisse (and her cat, Diablo) had arrived for an extended visit, Matisse considered the case open and shut.

The old lady demurred, however, taking the position that her "*Petit Diablo*"
could never have committed such an act. Infuriated, Matisse painted
these three canvases – originally entitled, *Things Were This Way, Then So,
And Finally Thus*. The entire tryptich was subtitled *An Explanation of
the Obvious for the Instruction of the Idiotic*. Aunt Clarisse cut her visit short –
and subsequently, history tells us, did the same for her will.

In his personal life,
the great impressionist Claude Monet
was a man of simple pleasures.
His favorite pipe; a stroll in his garden at Giverny;
a quiet hour with a good book and his calico, Montaigne,
purring in his lap: these meant far more to him
than the cafes and salons of Paris.
As they approached their declining years
together, however, Monet's absentmindedness and
Montaigne's wanderlust (and pranksterism)
increased more or less in parallel,
often resulting in episodes of fruitless
search such as the one pictured.

No painter in history has received greater sums of money for his work during his own lifetime than Picasso. Still, however rich he became, his lifelong penuriousness never lessened. When he found that a 25-peso bouquet of common wildflowers he had bought from a street vendor (it having been marked down from 75, and he having haggled further until he actually paid only 15) had been ruined by his wife's cat, which Picasso already perceived as eating him out of house and home, his fury was boundless. However, finding no market for this graphic record of the incident, he later repainted it, producing the symbol of love and harmony with which we are all familiar.

Matisse claimed that he was able to distill the essence of a subject's personality by projecting himself into the minds and souls of his models, and this painting seems to be a prime example of the typical result. It is described in an entry in his diary dated September 7, 1950.

My neighbor's cat sat motionless on the porch, transfixed by a nearby group of birds scratching about the lawn. I set out to project myself into the soul of the cat – to actually become the cat, if only for a moment. Suddenly I wanted to dance like the wind, to dip and soar and sing like a living flute. When I came to myself, I had a great craving to eat a junebug or an earthworm. It was then I realized I had missed the cat and projected myself into one of the birds...but the painting was already done, so what the hell.

James McNeill Whistler is almost as famous as an acerbic, misanthropic wit as a painter, and the reason is not hard to find. His mother, with whom he lived until well into his thirties, was widely acknowledged as the most disagreeable woman east of Philadelphia. Whistler tried desperately to win her approval, painting portrait after portrait and showering her with gifts, including the kitten pictured here. On the occasion of his last known visit to his mother's house, he asked, "*Ma mère*, is its cuteness not on the threshold of the excruciating?" She replied, "I would prefer that it, and you, would forbear to cross certain thresholds." Which, thereafter, they did.

One of the few commissions van Gogh ever received came from the proprietor of an unfashionable and unfrequented cafe on the outskirts of Paris. The offer of 25 francs for an advertising poster carried one proviso: it must include the cafe's cat, Laura, whose lissome charm (the owner believed) attracted customers. Van Gogh studied Laura for weeks, becoming fascinated by the ephemeral grace which seemed to enable her to be in several places at once, and he included this impression in his painting. When he presented the final canvas, the delusional restaurateur flew into a rage. "What are all these cats, jumping on tables, crawling everywhere – who would come to such a cafe? Your picture is a lie – I have but one cat!" Van Gogh, whose life experience fully prepared him to be unpaid for his efforts, said, "In fact, my painting is a greater lie than you think. For though you have fewer cats than I have shown, at least you have one – and you will notice that I have also painted in some customers."

For decades, critics and patrons alike have debated
the true meaning of Munch's famous depiction of suicidal
despair. As a result of this scrutiny, many previously unknown
(or painted-over) versions have come to light, somewhat
lessening the impact of what has generally been

believed to be a spontaneous outpouring of passionate angst.

According to recently translated notebooks, Munch was actually

attempting to develop a popular series – a comic strip, in fact –

which was to be entitled, "*Macht es Dich Nicht Verruckt?*"

("Don't You Just Hate It When This Happens?")

As widely celebrated as is the power of Picasso's better-known canvas, *Guernica*, discerning critics maintain that this is actually the superior work, involving as it does so many layers of subtle symbolism. Even the deceptively direct title, *Cat Coughing Up a Hairball*, is full of sly innuendo. Some believe the cat symbolizes postwar Europe, and the hairball the fascists. Others, citing Picasso's communist leanings, say the cat is Marx's Historical Imperative and the hairball is the decadent bourgeosie. Still others, who believe that Picasso had renounced communism by this time, claim that the cat is Spain and Franco is the hairball. Whatever the true interpretation, it is clearly a work of vision and passion, and all critics agree on one thing: it cannot be what Picasso insisted it was – just a picture of a cat coughing up a hairball.

The better-known version of this painting by Edward Hopper – the one with the human customers – has been the subject of endless speculation. Why are the two men dressed identically? Why do the three people seem unaware of each other's existence? What time is it supposed to be? – and so on. The explanation, though admittedly unusual, is simple: it seems that the owner of Kittie's All-Nite Diner, culinary jewel of Milford, Massachusetts, was a cat lover *in extremis*. Business being slow in the small hours, he wished to fete his feline friends in the style usually reserved for humans, but was hampered by Milford's oppressive laws regarding cats sitting on the counters of eating places. So he commissioned local artist Hopper to produce a few full-size likenesses of anthropoidal customers, and it is these cardboard cutouts – isolated, stiff, identical   that we see in the other version. This, on the other hand, is a picture of the true night life at Kittie's – the one beyond the view of the cops.

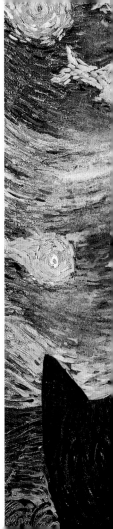

Many artists have had the apparent capacity to project themselves into the souls of their subjects (Matisse, as already noted, claimed this often), but van Gogh almost certainly leads this particular field. The downside, of course, for a mind as malleable and precariously balanced as van Gogh's, would have been the difficulty of subsequent extrication. This painting, *Fishy Fishy Night*, featuring the unmistakable silhouette of van Gogh's fourteenth cat, Syllabus, is dated June 8, 1889. In a letter to his brother Theo, dated August 2nd of the same year – almost two months later – van Gogh writes, "The common field mouse is a perfectly *gemütlich* substitute for the potato, and even superior, having...a greater variety of texture and being...only slightly harder to catch."

In the early 1920s, his diary tells us, René Magritte was just another struggling artist willing to take any commission that might earn a crust of bread. At about the same time, a certain obscure writer of children's verse was combing Europe in search of artists-for-hire, and their paths happened to cross. Magritte gladly accepted the assignment to illustrate a piece called *The Cat in the Hat* and produced this canvas within a few days. The writer (whose name, unfortunately, is never mentioned) rejected it, saying that the cat was only supposed to *wear* a hat, not actually be *in* one, but that he would give him another chance on a second story entitled *Green Eggs and Ham*. Magritte (who never took criticism very well) declined, on the grounds that the concept was a little too surreal for his taste.

Despite what many consider equally groundbreaking experiments in cubism and nonrepresentationalism, Duchamps never quite made the name for himself that his contemporary, Picasso, achieved. In fact, he had so much trouble making ends meet that he kept a sharp eye out for any chance to make a little cash, which is why he entered the poster contest sponsored by his local Ladies' Auxiliary Home Safety Committee. *Nude Descending a Staircase* was originally entitled *Watch Out for That Damn Cat*, but the Ladies' Auxiliary could make no more of it than the usual run of critics and patrons could make of Duchamps's other work. His poster did not place in the money.

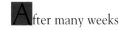After many weeks
of staring at his kitchen floor
in unseeing despair, Piet Mondrian
was suddenly seized by
inspiration for the new
Objectivist vision
that would make him famous.
Fluffy, who drew
his attention to the floor
in the first place,
remains uncredited.

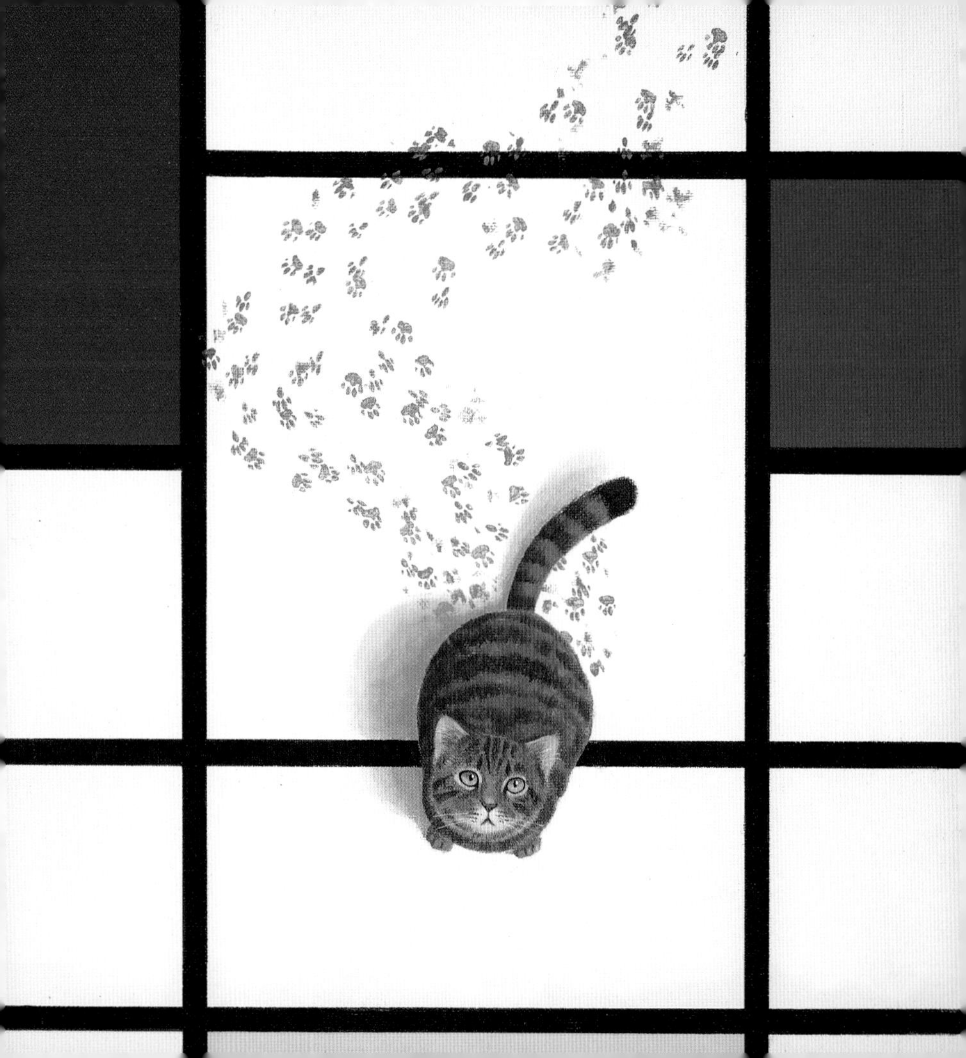

Whether cats and humans of similar temperament are drawn together from the beginning, or whether they simply take on shadings of each other's personalities over time, is unclear. One thing is certain, however: everyone in Arles knew whose cat Iris was.

As well regarded as M. C. Escher is by artists and collectors, he is perhaps even more widely admired by theoretical mathematicians, who are fascinated by his concrete representations of such abstract concepts as infinity, hypercubism, and dimensionality. One such mathematician met the artist at a trade show in the early sixties (Escher was pushing some mathematically sophisticated black-light posters at the time) and asked him if he could articulate his definition of infinity. "Easily," said Escher. "It's the time it takes you to cross the living room from the moment you first notice your cat has discovered the Christmas tree."

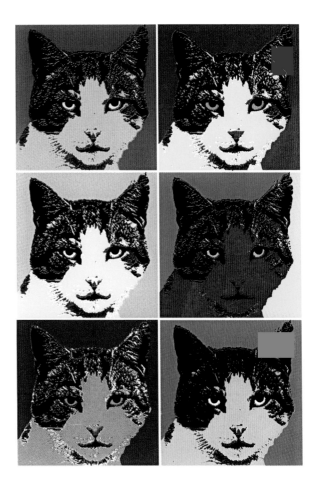

By the mid-1960s, Andy Warhol was the embodiment of the cutting edge in American art – and a rich man. While he was financially more than capable of owning the latest in photocopying technology, he was mechanically incapable of operating it. When his cat, Eisenhower, disappeared, he made a simple, artistically unpretentious poster which he intended to copy and staple to telephone poles around the neighborhood. The results, while maddening, were interesting enough – such as this example, later hand-colored with Magic Markers – to lead to his next major exhibition. Eisenhower turned out to be locked in the laundry room.

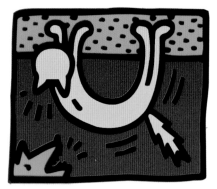

Many now-famous artists, in their struggling days, worked in other fields to keep body and soul together. Keith Haring, after stints as a McDonald's assistant manager, parking meter change collector, and frozen turkey truck driver, took a shot at being a Warner Bros. animator (he had a deep affection for Road Runner cartoons). Though he was not hired – they were unimpressed by his handling of their standard test, *Animating a Cat in Four Funny Situations* – he was able, some years later, to sell his rejected cel for enough money to buy a sprawling estate once owned by Cecil B. DeMille.

Including mineral rights.

For all his well-documented foibles, Vincent van Gogh personifies the passion of the artist. He attacked his subjects, often painting so furiously that his work incorporated changes that took place before his eyes – a sudden flock of birds, a chance traveler, and so on. This would seem to explain the inclusion in this case of his thirteenth cat, Jamais, who was apparently unable to resist passing through the still life arrangement. On the other hand, van Gogh was also notorious for misplacing his glasses, and Jamais rather resembles a sunflower.

Gustav Klimt's images of lush
sensuality are generally interpreted
as representations of the subjugation of
one's self to a lover. This less well-known
painting, however, makes it clear that
Klimt's ultimate statement was a bit
farther-reaching: if you *really* want to
subjugate your sense of self,
get a cat.

When they heard that *Cats of the Masters*, our modest entry in the field of art-oriented literature, was to contain many revelations about such giants as Rembrandt, van Gogh, and Picasso, the Grant Wood Preservation Society decided to reveal to us a secret they had kept for fifty years or more: there was a first, suppressed version of Mr. Wood's best-known image, *American Gothic*, entitled *What Shall We Do with the Dead Polecat?* Now, our editors may be city folk, but they are not fools. First, a polecat is not a cat, but a skunk (*Mephitis mephitis*). Second, the expired creature held aloft by the stolid tiller of the earth is clearly not a polecat, or any sort of cat at all, but an opossum (*Didelphis marsupialis*). Despite such blatant disqualifications, we include it within these pages so that we may not seem to be unsympathetic to the society's complaint that this particular painting of Mr. Wood's has suffered from unfair neglect and lack of exposure.

In the early years of the century, Georgia O'Keeffe carried on a long, and mostly long-distance, relationship with famed photographer Alfred Stieglitz. Alfred was a cat person, and Georgia sent many paintings of cats from her desert home to Manhattan. She, on the other hand, was a flower and cow skull person, and Alfred sent her photographs of as many similar things as he could find in New York. This seems to have been fine for a while, but as the bloom faded from the romance, each became increasingly critical of the other's gifts. In one – perhaps their last – exchange, O'Keeffe wrote, "It is beyond me why, when you know I want lilies and cow skulls, I consistently get fire hydrants and taxicab bumpers." Stieglitz replied, "At least when I photograph a fire hydrant, it resembles a fire hydrant. What is beyond *me* is how all your paintings of cats manage to look like flowers."

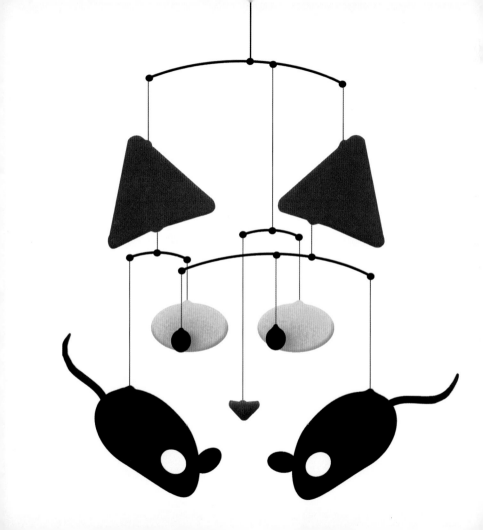

Alexander Calder's work often consisted of delicate shapes and balances rendered in that least delicate of materials, cast iron. When this mobile was first exhibited, Calder was asked what motivated him to attempt to capture the fluid grace of a cat in his hard and unforgiving medium. He said, "Cat? Oh, yeah...I guess if you squint it does sort of look like a cat."